FRANCIS FRITH'S

NORFOLK BROADS PHOTOGRAPHIC MEMORIES

THE FRANCIS FRITH COLLECTION

www.francisfrith.com

Francis Frith's

Norfolk Broads

Ormesby, The Broad near the Tea Rooms c1926 078008

Photographic Memories

Francis Frith's
Norfolk Broads

Elizabeth Purdy

First published in hardback in the United Kingdom in 2002 by
Frith Book Company Ltd
ISBN 1-85937-486-7

Paperback Edition 2005
ISBN 1-84589-073-6

British Library Cataloguing in Publication Data

Francis Frith's Norfolk Broads
Elizabeth Purdy

Frith Book Company Ltd
Frith's Barn, Teffont,
Salisbury, Wiltshire SP3 5QP
Tel: +44 (0) 1722 716 376
Email: info@francisfrith.co.uk
www.francisfrith.co.uk

Printed and bound in Great Britain

Front Cover: ORMESBY, The Broad near the Tea Rooms c1926 078008

Acknowledgements

I should like to thank the following for their valuable help:
The Broads Authority
Pat Davies
The many interesting people I met on my travels round the Broads

AS WITH ANY HISTORICAL DATABASE THE FRITH ARCHIVE IS CONSTANTLY BEING CORRECTED AND IMPROVED AND THE PUBLISHERS WOULD WELCOME INFORMATION ON OMISSIONS OR INACCURACIES

Contents

Francis Frith: *Victorian Pioneer*

FRANCIS FRITH, Victorian founder of the world-famous photographic archive, was a complex and multi-talented man. A devout Quaker and a highly successful Victorian businessman, he was both philosophical by nature and pioneering in outlook.

By 1855 Francis Frith had already established a wholesale grocery business in Liverpool, and sold it for the astonishing sum of £200,000, which is the equivalent today of over £15,000,000. Now a very rich man, he was able to indulge his passion for travel. As a child he had pored over travel books written by early explorers, and his fancy and imagination had been stirred by family holidays to the sublime mountain regions of Wales and Scotland. 'What lands of spirit-stirring and enriching scenes and places!' he had written. He was to return to these scenes of grandeur in later years to 'recapture the thousands of vivid and tender memories', but with a different purpose. Now in his thirties, and captivated by the new science of photography, Frith set out on a series of pioneering journeys to the Nile regions that occupied him from 1856 until 1860.

Intrigue and Adventure

He took with him on his travels a specially-designed wicker carriage that acted as both dark-room and sleeping chamber. These far-flung journeys were packed with intrigue and adventure. In his life story, written when he was sixty-three, Frith tells of being held captive by bandits, and of fighting 'an awful midnight battle to the very point of surrender with a deadly pack of hungry, wild dogs'. Sporting flowing Arab costume, Frith arrived at Akaba by camel sixty years before Lawrence, where he encountered 'desert princes and rival sheikhs, blazing with jewel-hilted swords'.

During these extraordinary adventures he was assiduously exploring the desert regions bordering the Nile and patiently recording the antiquities and peoples with his camera. He was the first photographer to venture beyond the sixth cataract. Africa was still the mysterious 'Dark Continent', and Stanley and Livingstone's historic meeting was a decade into the future. The conditions for picture taking confound belief. He laboured for hours in his wicker dark-room in the sweltering heat of the desert, while the volatile chemicals fizzed dangerously in their trays. Often he was forced to work in remote tombs and caves where conditions were cooler. Back in London he exhibited his photographs and was 'rapturously cheered' by members of the Royal Society. His reputation as a photographer was made overnight. An eminent modern historian has likened their impact on the population of the time to that on our own generation of the first photographs taken on the surface of the moon.

Venture of a Life-Time

Characteristically, Frith quickly spotted the opportunity to create a new business as a specialist publisher of photographs. He lived in an era of immense and sometimes violent change. For the poor in the early part of Victoria's reign work was a drudge and the hours long, and people had precious little free time to enjoy themselves. Most had no transport other than a cart or gig at their disposal, and had not travelled far beyond the boundaries of their own town or village. However, by the 1870s, the railways had threaded their way across the country, and Bank Holidays and half-day Saturdays had been made obligatory by Act of Parliament. All of a sudden the ordinary working man and his family were able to enjoy days out and see a little more of the world.

With characteristic business acumen, Francis Frith foresaw that these new tourists would enjoy having souvenirs to commemorate their days out. In 1860 he married Mary Ann Rosling and set out with the intention of photographing every city, town and village in Britain. For the next thirty years he travelled the country by train and by pony and trap, producing fine photographs of seaside resorts and beauty spots that were keenly bought by millions of Victorians. These prints were painstakingly pasted into family albums and pored over during the dark nights of winter, rekindling precious memories of summer excursions.

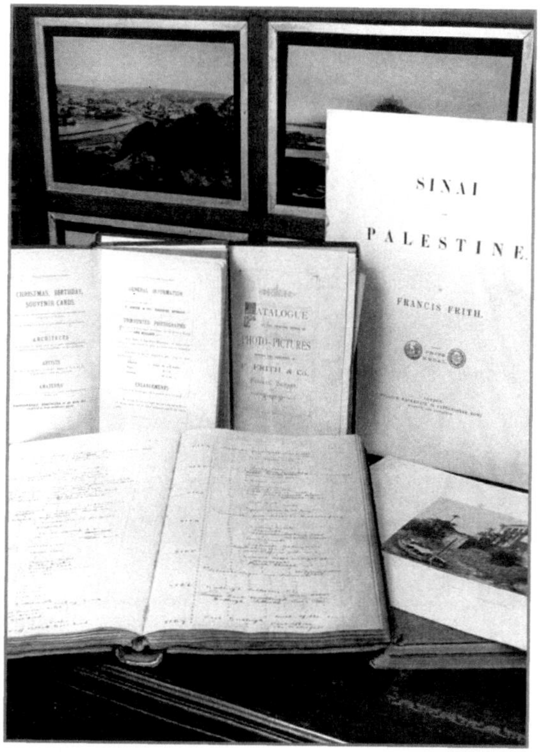

The Rise of Frith & Co

Frith's studio was soon supplying retail shops all over the country. To meet the demand he gathered about him a small team of photographers, and published the work of independent artist-photographers of the calibre of Roger Fenton and Francis Bedford. In order to gain some understanding of the scale of Frith's business one only has to look at the catalogue issued by Frith & Co in 1886: it runs to some 670 pages, listing not only many thousands of views of the British Isles but also many photographs of most European countries, and China, Japan, the USA and Canada – note the sample page shown on page 9 from the hand-written *Frith & Co* ledgers detailing pictures taken. By 1890 Frith had created the greatest specialist photographic publishing company in the

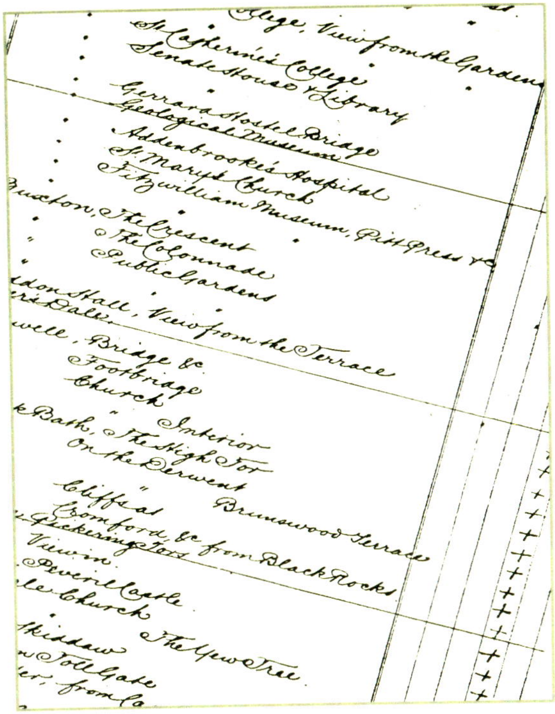

world, with over 2,000 outlets – more than the combined number that Boots and WH Smith have today! The picture on the right shows the *Frith & Co* display board at Ingleton in the Yorkshire Dales (left of window). Beautifully constructed with a mahogany frame and gilt inserts, it could display up to a dozen local scenes.

Postcard Bonanza

The ever-popular holiday postcard we know today took many years to develop. In 1870 the Post Office issued the first plain cards, with a pre-printed stamp on one face. In 1894 they allowed other publishers' cards to be sent through the mail with an attached adhesive halfpenny stamp. Demand grew rapidly, and in 1895 a new size of postcard was permitted called the court card, but there was little room for illustration. In 1899, a year after Frith's death, a new card measuring 5.5 x 3.5 inches became the standard format, but it was not until 1902 that the divided back came into being, with address and message on one face and a full-size illustration on the other. *Frith & Co* were in the vanguard of postcard development, and Frith's sons Eustace and Cyril continued their father's monumental task, expanding the number of views offered to the public and recording more and more places in Britain, as the coasts and countryside were opened up to mass travel.

Francis Frith died in 1898 at his villa in Cannes, his great project still growing. The archive he created continued in business for another seventy years. By 1970 it contained over a third of a million pictures of 7,000 cities, towns and villages. The massive photographic record Frith has left to us stands as a living monument to a special and very remarkable man.

Frith's Archive: *A Unique Legacy*

FRANCIS FRITH'S legacy to us today is of immense significance and value, for the magnificent archive of evocative photographs he created provides a unique record of change in 7,000 cities, towns and villages throughout Britain over a century and more. Frith and his fellow studio photographers revisited locations many times down the years to update their views, compiling for us an enthralling and colourful pageant of British life and character.

We tend to think of Frith's sepia views of Britain as nostalgic, for most of us use them to conjure up memories of places in our own lives with which we have family associations. It often makes us forget that to Francis Frith they were records of daily life as it was actually being lived in the cities, towns and villages of his day. The Victorian age was one of great and often bewildering change for ordinary people, and though the pictures evoke an impression of slower times, life was as busy and hectic as it is today.

We are fortunate that Frith was a photographer of the people, dedicated to recording the minutiae of everyday life. For it is this sheer wealth of visual data, the painstaking chronicle of changes in dress, transport, street layouts, buildings, housing, engineering and landscape that captivates us so much today. His remarkable images offer us a powerful link with the past and with the lives of our ancestors.

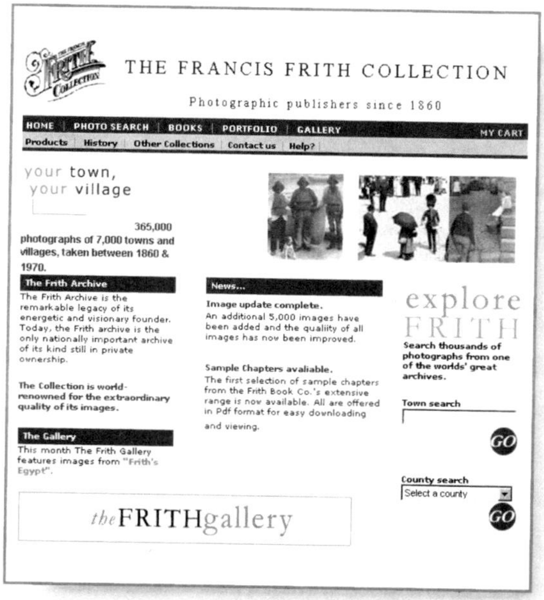

See Frith at www.francisfrith.co.uk

Today's Technology

Computers have now made it possible for Frith's many thousands of images to be accessed almost instantly. In the Frith archive today, each photograph is carefully 'digitised' then stored on a CD Rom. Frith archivists can locate a single photograph amongst thousands within seconds. Views can be catalogued and sorted under a variety of categories of place and content to the immediate benefit of researchers.

Inexpensive reference prints can be created for them at the touch of a mouse button, and a wide range of books and other printed materials assembled and published for a wider, more general readership - in the next twelve months over a hundred Frith local history titles will be published! The day-to-day workings of the archive are very different from how they were in Francis Frith's time: imagine the herculean task of sorting through eleven tons of glass negatives as Frith had to do to locate a particular sequence of pictures! Yet the archive still prides itself on maintaining the same high standards of excellence laid down by Francis Frith, including the painstaking cataloguing and indexing of every view.

It is curious to reflect on how the internet now allows researchers in America and elsewhere greater instant access to the archive than Frith himself ever enjoyed. Many thousands of individual views can be called up on screen within seconds on one of the Frith internet sites, enabling people living continents away to revisit the streets of their ancestral home town, or view places in Britain where they have enjoyed holidays. Many overseas researchers welcome the chance to view special theme selections, such as transport, sports, costume and ancient monuments.

We are certain that Francis Frith would have heartily approved of these modern developments in imaging techniques, for he himself was always working at the very limits of Victorian photographic technology.

The Value of the Archive Today

Because of the benefits brought by the computer, Frith's images are increasingly studied by social historians, by researchers into genealogy and ancestory, by architects, town planners, and by teachers and schoolchildren involved in local history projects.

In addition, the archive offers every one of us an opportunity to examine the places where we and our families have lived and worked down the years. Highly successful in Frith's own era, the archive is now, a century and more on, entering a new phase of popularity.

The Past in Tune with the Future

Historians consider the Francis Frith Collection to be of prime national importance. It is the only archive of its kind remaining in private ownership and has been valued at a million pounds. However, this figure is now rapidly increasing as digital technology enables more and more people around the world to enjoy its benefits.

Francis Frith's archive is now housed in an historic timber barn in the beautiful village of Teffont in Wiltshire. Its founder would not recognize the archive office as it is today. In place of the many thousands of dusty boxes containing glass plate negatives and an all-pervading odour of photographic chemicals, there are now ranks of computer screens. He would be amazed to watch his images travelling round the world at unimaginable speeds through network and internet lines.

The archive's future is both bright and exciting. Francis Frith, with his unshakeable belief in making photographs available to the greatest number of people, would undoubtedly approve of what is being done today with his lifetime's work. His photographs, depicting our shared past, are now bringing pleasure and enlightenment to millions around the world a century and more after his death.

Norfolk Broads - *An Introduction*

EAST ANGLIA LIES on the east coast of England, jutting into the North Sea. It is a wide-open country, with low horizons, bare to the winds blowing unhindered from the north pole and from the Ural mountains in the east. With its long, sandy beaches, it was an easy landing for invaders from the mainland of Europe, the Saxons and Danes and Angles, who gave their name to the area.

The Broads is a general term used to refer to that area of Norfolk and the part of Suffolk bordering the river Waveney, through which three main rivers connect shallow lakes known as broads. Water dominates the landscape, sometimes as vast open stretches reflecting a great arc of sky, sometimes as a swiftly-flowing river, sometimes as almost secret dykes providing drainage for the water-logged marshland.

Until 1965 it had been thought that the broads were the remains of flooding of the low-lying land by the sea. When the sea level dropped at the end of Roman times, these stretches of open water were left behind in the alluvial plains. Another theory was that broads originated as 'broadenings' of the rivers, which then altered course and left the lakes virtually isolated.

However, following extensive examination of cores taken from the beds of broads in the 1950s and 60s, it was proved conclusively that it was the extraction of peat for fuel which created these shallow pits. For a thousand years after the Romans abandoned the country in about 400 AD, East Anglia was the most heavily populated part of Britain. By the end of the 12th century, much of the fuel-providing woodland had been cleared from the area

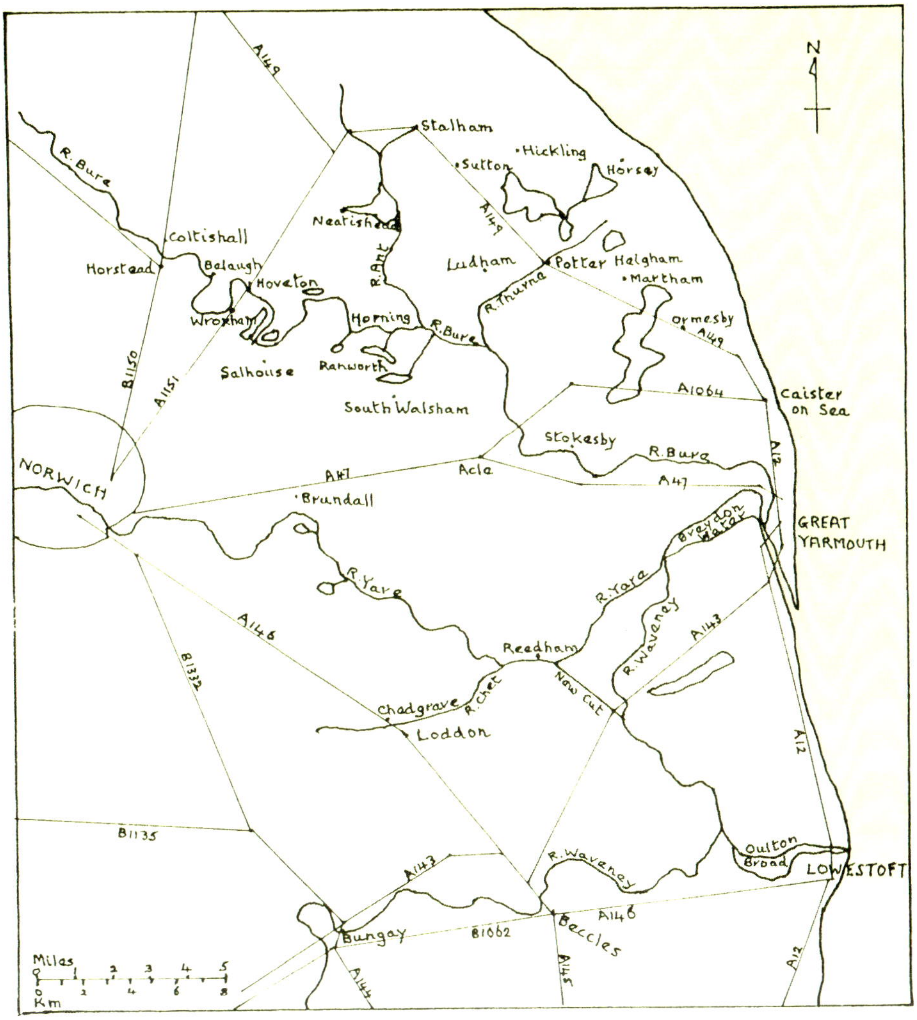

east of Norwich to the sea. An alternative fuel was found in the deep layer of peat, which had been laid down as a result of centuries of alluvial deposits and the decay of vegetation. Historical records indicate that peat extraction was a major industry between the 12th and 15th centuries, by which time many of the pits had flooded to form broads. The vertical sides of the broads, the shallowness of the water (in some places merely three or four feet above the clay floor) and the many 'islands' or peninsulas of undug peat stretching into the water confirm this theory.

Although the broads were formed independently of the river system, most are adjacent to the three main rivers, to which they are connected by short waterways - these provided the means of transporting the peat. The longest river, the Bure, flows roughly south-east. It is continuously navigable from Coltishall until it enters the North Sea at Yarmouth. The Bure's two tributaries, the Ant and the Thurne, flow south and south-west respectively, and together give access to the majority of broads. The upper reaches are through gentle water meadows, with plenty of trees and alder carr to give a softness to the undulating countryside.

The Wensum, flowing as an artery through Norwich, joins the Yare east of the city. The Yare travels first past nature reserves at Surlingham and beside Wheatfen, a wonderful haven for wildlife, and thence to the open expanse of Halvergate marshes down to join the Bure and Waveney through Breydon Water and out to its mouth at Great Yarmouth. The Yare is unbridged between Norwich and Yarmouth, and the only means of crossing the fast-flowing river is by the chain ferry at Reedham, an isolated spot of civilisation just beyond the point where the river Chet flows in.

The Waveney has traditionally been a boundary between the North folk and the South folk, separating the gently-rolling country of Norfolk, with its flint and brick houses, from the more undulating land of Suffolk, with its pink-washed, timber-frame buildings. Oulton Broad is the only broad directly accessible from the Waveney, but a cut between St Olave's (where the Bell Inn claims to be the oldest recorded inn in Broadland) and Reedham provides a route to the Yare and up to Norwich.

Until the railways were built early in the 19th century, the rivers provided vital trading routes for the transport of goods up from Yarmouth to Norwich (the stone for Norwich Cathedral had been brought from Caen in Normandy by this route), to Beccles, on the Suffolk border, and to North Norfolk via Aylsham. Navigation beyond Coltishall ceased in 1912, when a tremendous rainfall destroyed locks higher up: my father-in-law had to row across the flood to rescue passengers marooned in a train at Aylsham station. Trading up the Yare to Norwich continued up to the 1980s.

The maintenance of the rivers as navigation routes is one of the prime objectives of the Broads Authority, which has equivalent status to a National Park and which is responsible for maintaining a careful balance between the interests of all the varied activities of the Broads. Tourism has become a major industry, but its expansion must not be permitted to destroy the environment which attracts it. The conservation and development of one of the most important wetlands in Europe, and support for agriculture and those who live and work in the area, all contend for attention and resources.

A healthy river has banks protected from erosion by reed fens, which are such a beautiful characteristic of the Broads. They act as cushions against the wash of motor cruisers, and also as refuges for small mammals and for birds such as the redshank. Problems have been caused by nutrients leaching into the water, which encourages the proliferation of fast-growing plants, which can crowd out more delicate species. Seedling alders and birch, with shrubby undergrowth of currants, brambles, buckthorn and guelder rose, quickly form carr woodland and destroy the habitats of those insects, mammals and plants which thrive on the open marshland. Over 250 plant species are found in the Broads: many, such as the fen orchid, are unique to the area, and there are sedges, rushes and ferns which are rare elsewhere. The Norfolk hawker, the chaser dragonfly, and the emerald damselfly are spotted by enthusiasts, while the increasingly rare bittern, the marsh harrier, herons and snipe are sought by bird-watchers.

Each type of water environment, rivers and broads, fens and carr woodland, drained marshland and estuary, has its own wildlife and its own beauty. Careful management has to be exercised to ensure nature's balance.

Agriculture is a major industry in Norfolk, and the land surrounding the broads is some of the richest in the country. Both corn and root crops (particularly sugar beet) grow well. From its harvesting in late autumn, mounds of beet can be seen awaiting transport by lorry to the factory at Cantley, south of Acle. From December to March a great plume of white smoke from the tall chimneys is visible across the marshes from Yarmouth to Norwich, and even to Beccles, reminding us that work continues throughout the year.

Reeds for thatching are an important crop, and many beautiful examples of the thatcher's skill can be seen on local buildings. Grown at the water's edge, the grass is harvested during the winter, when bundles can be seen awaiting collection along the banks. Marsh hay is not grown as extensively as it was when harvesting by hand was viable - during the 19th century it was an important source of fodder for many of the horses crowding the streets of London.

Drained marshes provide excellent grazing for cattle, horses and some sheep, while the dykes give a plentiful supply of fresh water. The peaceful, low-lying landscape is dotted with drainage mills; a few are still powered by wind, but many more have been allowed to fall into decay and have been replaced by electric or diesel pumps.

In the 1980s, European Union agricultural policies encouraged farmers to turn from dairy to arable farming. One effect was the draining of areas of marshland to increase opportunities to grow cereal crops, with devastating effects on wildlife. Not only were the valuable wetlands in danger of disappearing, but more roads, storage barns and grain driers were being built, and fertilisers and pesticides were leaching into the river system. The Broads Authority set up a panel to ensure regular contact between the different interests, and the value of this support was shown during the drought of 1992 in assistance to overcome the severe water shortage. The Broads Grazing Marshes Scheme has become the blueprint for other conservation areas throughout Europe.

Mention the Broads to many people, and they will conjure up a picture of sailing holidays, or, more probably, of exploring the rivers of south Norfolk in a hired motor cruiser. Tourism is an important but largely a seasonal industry; between April and October the roads and villages fill with visitors. Unlike many lake districts, there are few places where a broad can be enjoyed from the road. It is not possible to drive round a broad, and boats can moor only at designated points. This is because in most cases, the banks are inaccessible through the fringe of reedbeds or alder carr. During the winter, permanent residents are busy building and refurbishing boats, repairing nature trails and hides, painting buildings, preparing educational courses and information for visitors, and training guides and wardens.

When the visitor comes to hire a vessel, he receives careful instruction, not only on managing the boat, but also about the regulations of the Broads. Speed limits are strictly enforced to ensure as little damage as possible is done to the banks and

the bed. A few broads are privately owned; generally these are important nature reserves especially rich in wildlife, and can only be entered with special permission.

At most of the larger villages it is possible to hire bicycles to explore the lanes and villages of broadland. Many are very isolated and unspoiled, but you will usually find a kindly welcome, a good pub or two and a beautifully-cared-for church to visit. There are many walks and water trails to follow from land or water. It is possible to sail right into the centre of Norwich, mooring alongside the Cathedral Close, and other towns and villages have museums, historic buildings and other points of interest.

Fishing for roach, rudd, bream, pike, perch and tench is permitted at designated points, but safety guidance should be followed. Swimming is not allowed in the rivers or broads, and the wearing of life jackets at all times is recommended, particularly by children. Sad to say, fatalities can occur, usually when someone slips into the water and is either caught by a current or becomes entangled in underwater weed.

The Broads Authority organises a programme of events during the season - canoeing, puppet shows, children's activity days and many others, as well as regular escorted tours. How Hill, a mansion in the Arts and Crafts style, stands proudly by the Ant, above Ludham, overlooking a wide expanse of broadland. Here the How Hill Trust runs educational courses for both adults and schoolchildren.

It is sad that it is now seldom possible to enjoy that traditional winter pleasure of ice skating. W A Dutt, writing in 1903, described the flooding of marshland with river water, enabling vast expanses of clear marsh ice to become highways. He remembered weeks on end when it was possible to skate on the broads, and a tale was told by an old man of how, as a young boy, he skated ten miles from Berney Arms to Yarmouth to buy a ha'pennyworth of yeast for his mother.

The photographs which follow are from a collection taken by Francis Frith, his family and his employees. They show a tantalising glimpse of the Broads, but only a glimpse. There is much more to be seen and enjoyed - and for sheer magical beauty nothing can surpass the peace of the Broads in winter, when a heavy hoar frost glistens on skeleton trees overhanging the river bank and sparkling silver fronds of reeds shimmer against a clear blue winter sky. Do come and see for yourself.

The Upper Bure

The river meanders through rich farmland from its source near Melton Constable eastwards to Aylsham, a pleasant market town, with an interesting church, founded by John of Gaunt, and a mainly Georgian market place. Trees are plentiful, and several stretches of the river are stocked with trout. Swans, ducks and geese are among the abundant wildlife to be seen. Water meadows border the river through Itteringham, Ingworth, Aylsham, Burgh, Buxton and down to Coltishall, where navigation starts.

Coltishall

The village borders the river Bure and marks the end of the navigable waterway up from Yarmouth. It is set amid gently rolling, rich agricultural land where the main crops are corn and sugar beet. There are several shops selling basic necessities, one or two antique shops and several good pubs.

Coltishall, The River Bure 1902 48112
On the south side of Coltishall the river Bure flows gently through water meadows where cattle and horses graze. Since the 18th century, substantial houses have been built with gardens leading down to the river, alongside the main road which runs parallel to but out of sight of the river.

Coltishall, The Lock 1902 48122

This tranquil scene was destroyed in August 1912 when six inches of rain fell in twenty-four hours. The massive force of the great flood swept away the lock gates and undermined the foundations. Thereafter it was not possible for boats to travel higher up the Bure, and all traffic from the Broads now halts at Coltishall.

CONFECTIONER
LYONS TEA
WILLS'S
GOLD FLAKE
CIGARETTES
LYONS' TEA

Coltishall
The Village c1945
C417067

The nearest this long, straggling village has to a market square is a broadening of the Norwich to North Walsham road, beside which the War Memorial stands under chestnut trees. The front of the shop to the right is unchanged since Edwardian days and is now Coltishall Pharmacy, but the corner where the confectioner's small shop stood has been redeveloped and now houses Coltishall Antiques Centre.

Coltishall, The Village from the River c1955

C417053

The Rising Sun public house is ideally situated to refresh visitors who moor their boats alongside the well-kept common. The scene is little changed today, although summer sees boats, mostly fibreglass cruisers now, moored nose to tail and often two abreast, along this reach of the Bure. The houseboat has long since gone, as has Bullards Norwich brewery.

Horstead, The Mill and the Pond c1955

H343036

Cross the humped bridge over the river from Coltishall, and the village becomes Horstead. Until it was destroyed by fire in 1963, Horstead Mill processed locally-grown corn into flour and animal feed, which was then transported downstream by wherry. Mill owners are still responsible for operating the sluice gates to control flooding.

Horstead, The Mill Pool c1955 H343012
This is a tranquil sight on a sunny day, with the mill reflected in the peaceful water and myriads of buttercups flowering in the grass. Children fish for pike in the Mill Pool, and a man tries his luck by the mill race.

The Broads, The River Bure below Horstead House 1934 86401
In contrast to the flat marshes of the lower Bure, the upper reaches often have thick undergrowth and trees along the banks. This delightful scene near Coltishall shows a private garden bordering the river, with steps to enable the owners to alight from their boat. The boathouse can be seen further along the river.

Belaugh

Belaugh
The Church from the River c1955 B495004
A loop from the Coltishall to Wroxham road can take you down to the delightful small village of Belaugh. This view from the river shows almost the whole village, including the church of St Peter, whose tiny churchyard is a designated conservation area with particularly interesting ferns, lichens and flowers. The fine rood screen inside the church depicts the twelve apostles, whose faces were said, by a zealous Puritan, to have been obliterated by 'a godly trooper' during the Civil War.

Belaugh
Children Playing c1955 B495003
The staithe at Belaugh has been tidied since this picture was taken, and houses have been built on the land across the road. Boys wearing ties, jackets and short trousers, and girls with neat ankle socks and strap shoes are typical of school-age children of the 1940s and 50s.

Belaugh, The Bure 1934 86394
It is hard to imagine a more tranquil scene than this one, taken from Belaugh staithe. The peaceful stretch of the river Bure is the same today as it was 70 years ago.

Wroxham

Often called the Capital of the Broads, Wroxham is the largest village between Norwich and Yarmouth. Roy's, which claims to be the largest village store in the world, occupies most of the shopping area on the east side of the bridge with its many departments. This is technically Hoveton, Wroxham being the large residential area west of the river. A miniature railway runs between Wroxham and Aylsham, from where tourists can visit Blickling Hall, a National Trust property.

Wroxham, The Broad 1934 86359
On a dull day this large broad can appear a threatening expanse of rough, grey water, but it provides opportunities for excellent sailing. This amusing photograph shows a lady in mermaid-like pose seated on a tuft of reed.

LLOYDS
BANK
SHAPES
ROY

Wroxham
At Wroxham Bridge
c1955 W156145

We are looking towards Roys of Wroxham (on the Hoveton side of the bridge). The wooden building on the right has been demolished, but others remain. Lloyds Bank is now Ken's Fish Shop, and motor traffic congests the road even out of season, forcing pedestrians to cross the river via a separate footbridge. A fire in 1995 destroyed Roys main building, which has since been rebuilt.

Wroxham, The Bridge c1950 W156123

The bridge joining Wroxham to the west and Hoveton to the east was declared unsafe in the 1960s. A 'temporary' bridge was superimposed on the old stone structure, pending the building of a town bypass, which still has to be constructed. This photograph shows one of the last trading wherries with its high mast, which had to be lowered to pass under bridges.

Wroxham, The King's Head Staithe c1950 W156099

The variety of boats and number of boatsheds indicate the importance of Wroxham as a centre for holidaymakers. The King's Head Hotel now provides an attractive venue for a meal alongside the moorings, and is easily reached by rail from Norwich, Cromer or Aylsham. The station can be seen on the horizon right centre of the picture.

Wroxham
Bure Court c1940 W156109

This is a typical example of many luxury homes built in the first half of the 20th century which enabled owners to enjoy life beside the water. The roof is thatched with local reed, and the principal rooms are elevated to avoid floods and to afford excellent views of the waterways. An interesting balcony has steps down to the garden, where leisure furniture and croquet hoops indicate a relaxed way of life. A motor launch is tied up at the private mooring.

Wroxham
The Church 1921
70895

St Mary's church is now approached through a housing estate, but is well worth a visit to admire the magnificent Norman doorway as well as the contrasting simple but lovely modern screen at the west end.

Wall's
Ice Cream

Hoveton, The Village 1934 86363
A long-vanished view of Hoveton in the days of the horse and cart, the flaming torch sign for the school approach and the neatly thatched cottage. All have been replaced by sprawling residential streets and streams of cars.

Salhouse

Salhouse
The Broad and the River Bure 1902 48143
A small broad off the busy river Bure, Salhouse in 1902 displayed the tranquillity of the English countryside beloved by Victorian artists. A wherry with its square black sail travels up the river, while two men are rowing on the broad itself near the bundles of reeds.

Salhouse The Broad 1902 48147

A wonderful picture which shows Norfolk reeds in all stages of their growth and use: growing in the water, gathered into boats, and bundled and piled up to await transport further afield. A partially-thatched hut on the right of the picture, with a beautifully thatched cottage behind and another example of fine thatching on the building at the left show the ultimate use of nature's gift.

Salhouse
Boats on Salhouse Broad c1940 S47006
Woodland surrounds many of the broads in the upper stretches of the Bure, providing shelter and seclusion for these early cabin cruisers. The thick reed beds obscure the exact edge of the land.

Horning

Horning is a long village which has grown up between the A1062 and an attractive stretch of the Bure. There are several useful shops and plenty of places to eat alongside the river.

Horning
The 'Queen of the Broads' 1934 86371
A pleasure steamer, the 'Queen of the Broads', crowded with tourists and well equipped with life belts, ploughs her way round the wide bend of the river Bure and down towards the sea. A woman stands precariously on the deck of an early motor launch, but neither she nor the child is wearing a life jacket. Notice the corrugated iron boathouse on the right.

▼ **Horning, The Ferry 1934** 86370
Here we have a good view of the sweep of river which provides an extensive water frontage for Horning. The Ferry Boat Inn is on the right, with deck chairs awaiting guests, and on the left is the landing point for the ferry.

▼ **Horning, The Ferry c 1965** H116124
The punt-like chain ferry still plies between Horning village and Woodbastwick Nature Reserve. The ferryman on the right grips the guiding chain to steady the boat while a passenger disembarks, and a second passenger waits with his bicycle.

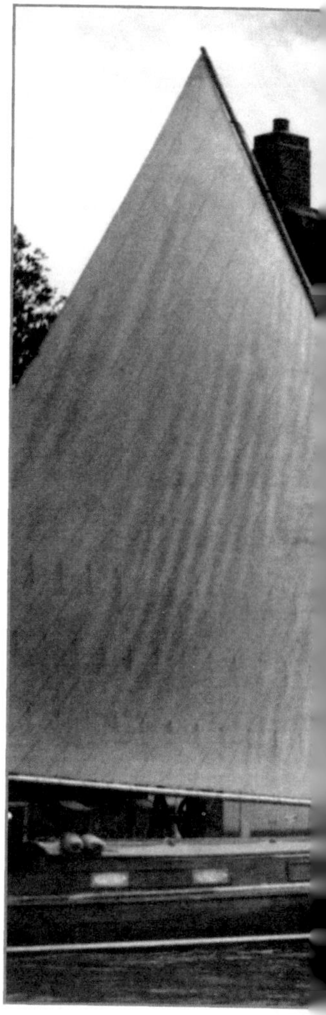

▲ **Horning, Ye Olde Ferry Inn c1965** H116114
The Ferry Inn has had a chequered history, having been bombed on 27 April 1941 when 42 people were killed. After being rebuilt in 1956, disaster again struck with a fire in 1965. Again it was rebuilt in the same style, but Norfolk tiles replace the thatched roof. The ghost of a middle-aged lady is said to haunt the inn, and several witnesses have smelt the candle she holds.

Horning Swan Reach 1934 86366
The Union Jack flies and boats are dressed with flags, and three girls watch intently as two yachts turn in the reach. Three ladies in hats and high heels consult papers. Could this be a race or regatta?

Horning
The River 1902 48109
Away from the busyness of Swan Reach, on a quiet stretch of the river Bure, two ladies in tight-bodiced dresses and hats in Edwardian fashion struggle with the oars of their rowing boat, while two men watch with concern. The tower of Horning church can be spotted among the trees.

Horning
The Swan c1965 H116103
An attractive garden borders the river in front of the Swan Hotel. Since 1965 an extension to the hotel has replaced the low building beside the thatched house. The village staithe is on the right of the picture, with a row of Georgian houses behind. The Dutch gable of the shop front is an architectural feature often seen in this part of the country - a legacy of frequent migrations of Dutch farmers and wool merchants from the Netherlands. To the left of the hotel, the road apparently entering the water is a public slipway for private boats.

Horning, The Village c1965 H116144
Horning main street runs parallel with the river. On the left is the rear of the Swan Inn; a car park has replaced the buildings ahead. Roys have been succeeded by Horning Main Stores, but the shop building still displays the interesting herringbone brickwork pediment.

Horning, The New Inn c1965 H116117
The front of this charming Georgian house, with its bay windows and portico at the front door, is now obscured by the addition of a single-storey annexe which provides a riverside eating area for customers.

Horning, The Petersfield House Hotel Moorings c1965 H116137
High above the river stands the Petersfield House Hotel, whose guests are able to relax by the summer house under the chestnut tree. A path and lawns now lead from the hotel to the mooring.

Horning, A Mansion on the Bure c1965 H116107
Overlooking the river Bure stands a large, thatched house in the Arts and Crafts style, typical of many built between the wars. Well-tended gardens lead down to a private mooring and boat houses. This property has the added attraction of a waterside summer house.

Ranworth

Ranworth
The Broad 1934 86389
It is a busy day for the small Ranworth Broad, with sailing boats and dinghies out as well as a large motor cruiser. In the centre of the picture is a sailing wherry, the shallow, wide bottomed boat with its characteristic square sail, an adaptation of the traditional trading wherry.

Ranworth
The Broad c1930 R9003
Here a young girl throws crumbs to a family of ducks, a popular pastime for holiday makers. On the right of the group, three young ducklings are hitching a ride on their mothers' backs. Reed beds can be clearly seen at the far edge of the broad, with trees on land behind.

Ranworth, The Staithe c1945 R9047
Bundles of Norfolk reed lie stacked at the edge of Ranworth staithe awaiting collection by thatchers. The Maltsters Inn can be seen across the road. The flint walled boatshed on the left is now obscured by a gift shop/information centre.

Ranworth, Approach to the Broad c1955 R9051
A brick-built cottage on the lane leading to the broad has an unusual herringbone pattern on the ridge of its thatched roof. The casement windows are the traditional style in Norfolk cottages. An abundance of wild flowers covered the hedgerows before spraying or cutting became common practice.

Ranworth, The Church 1934 86390
One of the most beautiful of the many lovely Broads churches is St Helens at Ranworth, a short walk from the staithe. The road has widened little since 1934, and there is now a small area where two or three cars can park. The owners of the old-fashioned bicycles propped against the fence are working on the verge opposite.

Ranworth, The Church, the Rood Screen 1934 86391
The mid 15th-century rood screen is considered by many to be the finest in the country, having escaped damage by Cromwell's troops. A major restoration in 1960 revealed beautifully-coloured portraits of apostles and saints. The font and lectern are both noteworthy, and a mediaeval antiphoner in superb condition is on display. If you feel energetic, a climb to the roof of the tower will reward you with a magnificent view over broadland.

South Walsham

The Broads 1902 48161
This lovely photograph shows a broad on the upper Bure, possibly South Walsham, showing water lilies which were common on many broads early in the 20th century. A private boathouse on the left is constructed of wood and thatch.

South Walsham, The Broad 1902 48134
The lawn of a country house sweeps down to the water; a pile of mown grass can be seen on the right. The boat on the left, adjacent to the rather decrepit boatshed, has an awning to protect passengers from the harmful rays of the sun.

South Walsham, Harvest Scene 1902 48135
A charming but puzzling picture of three girls in a harvest field, wearing shawls and hats. What is the one on the right holding? The corn (oats?) has obviously been cut by hand and piled into small stacks to dry before threshing. But why was it not bundled neatly into stooks? The crop growing on the left appears to be reed.

The River Ant

The longer of the two tributaries of the Bure, the river Ant joins the broads waterway system at Dilham, and flows almost due south through open agricultural countryside to join the Bure just beyond Ranworth.

Wayford Bridge

Wayford Bridge
The Broads c1945 T213065
In 1363 there is a reference to 'Wardeforthebrigge' over the Ant. That was an age of great prosperity, thanks to the flourishing wool trade, and there is little sign of such wealth and population in the small hamlet of today. The old road bridge at Wayford Bridge was replaced towards the end of the 20th century by a fine, wide bypass. But the site of the old bridge and the cottages in this photograph can still be seen nearby.

Wayford Bridge, The River c1955 T213067
The river near the new bridge now has rows of wooden houseboats moored along the right bank, where Wayford Farm has been developed into the Wayford Bridge Hotel. There are more trees today, and the countryside looks less bleak.

Stalham

Stalham
The Mill and the Staithe c1955 S467032
The Museum of the Broads is now housed in the brick building with decorative arches alongside the staithe. It was formerly the Excise House, built in 1812, for customs officers to inspect imported goods arriving by wherry from Yarmouth. The centre arch with a door has been removed, leaving no trace on the outside brickwork, but it can be clearly seen inside the building.

Stalham
View from the Staithe c1955 S467048

Further along the staithe is a typical modern riverside bungalow with a neatly tended garden. Motor cruisers are moored along the public bank, and a young lad is quanting (a method of propelling by means of a pole, similar to punting) a dinghy along the shallow waterway.

Stalham, The Staithe c1955 S467055

This view of the staithe from the old Excise House shows Southgates Boat Hire office, which is now Rivercraft Yachting Services. The family butcher has gone, but the house belonging to Miss Teasel, a well-known local character, still overlooks her pretty garden. The shed on the right is an engine workshop.

Stalham, Sutton Cut on the Ant c1955 S467049

A tranquil evening scene showing the peace and solitude to be found in broadland as a yachtsman prepares for the night. This is one of the few sites where it is still possible to find otters.

Stalham, The Staithe c1955 S467052

In contrast, an evening scene further along the cut shows holidaymakers enjoying the company of other boat people whose boats are moored alongside. The dinghy on the left has an outboard motor - useful when one tires of rowing! The ornamental fish on the prow of the large motor cruiser is the emblem of the boatyard.

The Broads, Hunsett Mill c1945 T213034
Many windmills have now disappeared, and have been superseded by electric pumps. Hunsett Mill, near the top of the Ant, was constructed to drain the waterlogged ground to enable agricultural crops to be grown. It is still a popular landmark, though now accessible only through private property. The man on 'Rangoon' has moored his pleasure cruiser and balances his tripod and camera on the cabin roof to photograph the lovely old mill.

The Broads, Near Barton Staithe c1945 T213021
The Parish Staithe at Barton is a lovely backwater off the broad. It is owned by the Parish Council and provides 24-hour public mooring, but boat storage and other mooring is reserved for parishioners under a permit scheme. There are now more trees than appear in this photograph.

Neatishead, A Backwater N136005
Bundles of Norfolk reed are stacked on both banks of this shallow backwater. The growing of reeds provides one of the principal industries of the broads area. Note the shallow boats which are necessary to reach the reed beds.

Ludham

Ludham
The Village c1934 L110011
An overview of Ludham from the tower of St Catherine's Church shows the well-wooded, rich agricultural land surrounding the village before many of the hedges had been removed. The vehicle outside the kissing gate at the end of the church path is a 1920s model. The memorial cross at the corner of the churchyard commemorates those who fell in the 1914-18 war.

CATFIELD 2
CROMER 22

Ludham, Main Street c1955 L110072
Opposite Ludham Church an interesting row of thatched cottages adjoins two small Georgian houses, one with a slate roof and one with Norfolk tiles. The thatched dormer window has now been altered to match the other four, and the Alfresco Tearooms have replaced the shop with its fascinating display of old implements.

Ludham, A Spring Morning at the Staithe c1955 L110067
All is bustle as the boats are got ready for the day's activity. In the foreground a man rows his dinghy, and on the bank another prepares to board his boat, assisted by another man steadying it. The crews of the three motor launches are preparing their vessels, and in the background a sailing cruiser has already departed down river. The entrance to the Broad is on the right.

◄ **Ludham, The Village c1934** L110030

Old vehicles in the centre of Ludham village have their spare wheels attached to the side of the bonnet. The right-hand car has a 'dickey' seat at the back, closed in the photograph. The Kings Arms still caters for thirsty villagers, and the grocery store with its pull-out sun blind has now been replaced by Barnaby's Bistro.

▼ **Ludham The Mill 1934** 86377B

On the west bank of the Ant stood Ludham Mill, a tower mill 20ft high to the iron curb, with a base diameter of 12ft 4in, including 18in thick walls. It fell into disrepair, and now nothing remains of this fine landmark.

◄ **Ludham Womack Water c1955** L110061

Of interest to sailors is the most unusual clinker-built sailing boat, still moored but with sails already catching the breeze. In the centre of the picture two men are working on an another unusual boat, a motorised wherry - notice the shortened mast.

Horsey, The Church c1955 H341001

The small village of Horsey next the Sea has a delightful Saxon church which has succeeded in its fight to remain open. The lovely round tower is obscured by trees in this photograph, but it is still possible to admire the thatched roof and the stone finial on the east gable. Inside the church, it is interesting to notice the basket-weave reeds attached to the roof beams, forming a base for the outer thatching.

The River Thurne

The eastern tributary of the river Bure rises west of Waxham, not far from the sea, and flows south-west, joining Horsey Mere, Hickling Broad and Martham Broad into the broads system. It is bridged at Potter Heigham and joins the Bure at Thurne.

Martham, The Staithe c1955 M228030

A motor dinghy carries a boatload of adults and children past the pumping mill at Martham Staithe. Parent swans with three cygnets are a common sight on the Broads rivers, but many are killed by flying into overhead electricity wires. Holidaymakers enjoy tea in their moored yacht, while others prepare it in the garden of their bungalow.

Hickling
The Staithe c1945

T213044

Away from the broad, along the staithe, the moored boats can bob gently in the calmer water. In the background is the Pleasure Boat Inn, popular with visitors to the Broads.

Hickling
The Broad c1965
H307024
A large broad exposed to the cold east wind, Hickling can appear grey and unfriendly on a bleak day, but on sunny summer days it provides an exhilarating sail. The date, 1965, is clearly reflected by the clothes of bystanders - early, baggy jeans and headscarves.

Hickling

Hickling
The Staithe c1965
H307019
This photograph was taken from the Pleasure Boat Inn. The staithe had become much busier in the 20 years after the war. Motor cruisers were becoming larger and more numerous, almost crowding out the traditional sailing boats. The thatched boathouses in the background and on the left of the photograph are still in excellent repair, but a few of the trees have been felled.

Hickling
The Staithe c1955
H307009
The neatly-tended garden beside one of the thatched boathouses provides a vantage point to watch boats on the broad. Note the old tyres protecting the corner of the staithe.

Hickling, The Pleasure Boat Inn c1955 H307013

The Two-Necked Swan, as this inn was called in 1830, has blossomed into the Pleasure Boat Inn. Today the annexe shown on the right of the building has been rebuilt to accommodate a smart dining room, and the writing on the windows - typical in 1955 - has been removed. It is still a delightful waterside halt.

Hickling, The Broad c1965 H307028

A tranquil backwater off Hickling Broad shows privately-owned yachts at rest among the reeds. A mother is attending to two youngsters, while another child crosses from the boat to the dinghy, a potentially hazardous leap. That was 1965: today the wearing of a lifejacket would be automatic.

Potter Heigham

Potter Heigham is an important village, as it bridges the river Thurne.
It has become a major centre for boat building and hiring.

Potter Heigham
The River Thurne c1955 P167070
This general view of the river near Potter Heigham bridge clearly illustrates the flat and treeless banks of the river. The quay on the left is reserved for yacht moorings, and motor cruisers are required to tie up on the opposite bank.

◄ **Potter Heigham**
Quanting c1955

P167032

The shallowness of the river is apparent in this picture of a man quanting towards the iron railway bridge. The railway line has since closed.

Potter Heigham
The River Thurne c1926 P167028
In the foreground a trading wherry is shown in considerable detail. Another is berthed on the opposite bank, identifiable by the wide, shallow hull and very high pennanted mast. Cargoes were transported up country from Yarmouth by river wherries until the 1970s.

Potter Heigham
The Bridge 1934 86381
A pleasure cruiser has lowered its mast to enable it to pass under the stone and brick bridge with its wide central arch and two pointed side arches. It was a matter of pride amongst traditional boatmen - and required immense skill - to approach the bridge at full speed, reef the sail, lower the mast and emerge the other side without losing way.

Potter Heigham
The River c1955
P167058
A long-established boat builder, Herbert Woods, has extensive sheds alongside the river. The buildings look much the same today as in 1955. The square office block is a listed building, and when it became unsafe it had to be rebuilt in 2000 to a virtually identical design.

Potter Heigham, The Broads c1926 P167006
Here we see sailing boats and dinghies alongside the River Thurne, with G Applegate's boatbuilding sheds on the west bank. The Bridge Hotel, which here stands squarely in the background at the end of the footpath, burnt down in 1987 and has not been replaced.

The Broads, An Eel Catcher's Hut c1945 T213015
Eels used to be commonly found in the Broads rivers, but there is now only one hut remaining at Kandel Dyke above Potter Heigham. Notice the nets to the left of the hut.

Ormesby

South-east of Potter Heigham lie three broads outside the rivers system, Ormesby, Filby and Rollesby. A three-mile dyke, Muck Fleet, connects Filby Broad to the Bure, but it is not navigable. The main Yarmouth road now bypasses Ormesby St Margaret, which has returned to a quiet, charming village.

Ormesby
The War Memorial c1955 078001a
The war memorial stands at the central crossroads of Ormesby St Margaret. The fencing behind has now been removed, and an open, grassy area gives the village a heart. The petrol station on the right is now a large self-service garage.

Ormesby, The Broad near the Tea Rooms c1926 078008

The Eels Foot Inn now dispenses refreshments to visitors after their row on the broad. The ladies' headwear is typical of the early 1930s, and short skirts were in vogue. Motor cruisers are not common on Ormesby Broad, as it is not connected to the river system.

Ormesby
The Parish Church c1955 078006
St Margaret's Church has a fine Norman doorway; inside there are very interesting stained glass windows, including a beautiful modern one depicting St Margaret with the dragon. A clock was installed on the tower to celebrate the Millenium in 2000. The huge chestnut tree has disappeared, as has the garden where the children are playing.

Ormesby
The Broad 1891 28734
Unlike most broads, Ormesby is accessible by road rather than river and preserves a quietness not usually found during holiday periods. Thick reed beds glow golden in winter sunshine, a magical sight with blue sky reflected in the water.

The Lower Bure

From Acle to Yarmouth the Bure flows through the flat, low-lying Halvergate marshes. Cattle graze there, and wildlife is undisturbed, but there are few trees to break the cold east wind blowing over the reeds. Nevertheless, there is a natural beauty to be appreciated in the wide, open sky and the subdued colours of old marshmen's cottages and windmills reflected in streams and pools.

Acle

Acle, The Bridge c1929 A204036
One of the most frequently-painted sites on the Broads was the old Acle Bridge with its three arches, which we see here. The bridge has frequently been rebuilt - repairs were first recorded in 1101. It was rebuilt most recently in about 1930, and was replaced with a concrete model in 1989. A hire boat yard now occupies the site around the dyke where the dinghies are moored. The car and charabanc parked on the opposite bank show that Acle was an attraction for trippers between the wars.

▼ **Acle, The Bridge Hotel c1940** A204001
The painted advertisement for Bass on a window is the only indication that this farmhouse beside Acle bridge is an inn. The thatched roof has an unusual border above the edge, which reflects the pattern of the ridge. An early tractor stands in the yard.

▼ **Acle, The Bridge Inn c1955** A204098
By the mid 1950s, the Bridge Inn had a flint porch, thatched to match the roof. The area outside had been made into an attractive garden where refreshments purchased at the annexe could be enjoyed. Drain pipes and telephone wires indicate the arrival of modern conveniences. Today the annexe has lost its pretty little porch and become a souvenir gift shop, and the lawns and flower beds are a car park.

▲ **Acle, Eastick's Yacht Station c1929** A204019
The large hire-boat companies have taken over many of the small boat-building firms, and Easticks has now become Hoseasons. These sheds burnt down in about 1996. Holiday makers relaxing on the cabin cruiser in 1929 enjoyed a less crowded river than they would today.

Acle, The Staithe c1929
A204003
Out of season, all the wooden-hulled boats moored along the staithe are covered with protective tarpaulins. Two houseboats are moored near the boathouse, and a fisherman tries his luck from a dinghy.

◄ **The Broads**
The Greengrocer c1945
T213029
Below Acle bridge a provisioner brings supplies of fruit, vegetables, milk (in churns) and other essentials to holidaymakers and people living on houseboats such as this one on the right. Note the stone water jars at the rear of the houseboat.

Acle, Upton Dyke c1965 A204115

From Acle to Yarmouth the Bure flows through low-lying, flat marshland with few trees to break the skyline. As late as 1965 the great majority of boats are still sail, though some hulls are made of fibreglass.

The Broads, St Benet's Abbey Ruins c1945 T213023

A yacht in full sail races past a well-known landmark on the lower Bure, pulling its dinghy behind. A motor cruiser chugs its way along the north bank. Little remains of the Benedictine Abbey except this gateway, though traces can be found of the foundations (known by marshmen as groundsels) of the boundary wall and of a cruciform church. Here Sir John Fastolff, of Caister Castle, is buried.

The Broads St Benet's Abbey 1934 86379

The Abbey of St Benet-at-Holm was founded in 1020 AD by King Canute. It survived the dissolution of the monasteries, but Henry VIII transferred its income and its Abbot, William Rugge, to the see of Norwich. The Bishop of Norwich is still Abbot of St Benet's and holds a service at the abbey each August, arriving in a procession of boats.

◄ **Stokesby**
The Post Office
c1965 S469040
A modern mini-market now houses Stokesby Post Office, and the building shown here has become a candle maker's workshop and a tearoom with a charming garden beside the river. The elevation of the house has been altered to include a balcony and an extension on the left side.

Stokesby

Stokesby is another hidden gem of a village east of Acle on the north bank of the Bure, until relatively recently without a road.

Stokesby
The Ferry Inn c1955 S469015
A step away from the green by the staithe is the inn, which is now called the Stokesby Ferry. Beside the pavilion is the departure point from which the chain ferry used to transport passengers across the river. In 1940 both river and marshes froze, so it was possible to walk the whole way to Acle. The ferry became redundant when a road was built. The Provision Stores with its old-fashioned vending machine on the corner is now a private house.

Stokesby
A Wherry on the River c1955
S469020
A magnificent photograph of a trading wherry, with its square black sail and tall mast, on the Bure near Stokesby. The wide-hulled, shallow-draught boat was ideal for transporting goods up from Yarmouth. Only one original wherry remains, though replicas are now in use. Norfolk reeds are growing on the left of the river, while the right side shows the flat Halvergate marshes.

◄ **The Broads**
The 'Silver Swallow'
c1932 T213352

The River Yare

At Norwich, the Wensum joins the Yare to become part of the Broads river system. It flows through attractive countryside, which is wooded as far as Surlingham, and then flattens out into fenland. By the time the Yare reaches Reedham, where the river Chet flows in, the horizon is very low. The narrow road winds through wind-swept fields and marshes to the chain ferry, the only means of crossing the river during its 25-mile journey to the sea. Paintings by the 19th-century artists of the Norwich School, Crome, Cotman, Stannard and others, vividly depict the countryside east of Norwich.

Brundall

Brundall, Tidecrafts Yard c1960 B497003
Boatsheds on the right of the picture are typical of many, with mooring for several boats. A refuelling pump stands on the edge of the water next to a general stores. A wooden bungalow with its own mooring is similar to many bordering the rivers of the northern Broads.

The Broads
The 'Enchantress' c1932
T213354
These two motor cruisers were available for hire, and the photographs were probably produced for hire firms to use in their brochures. The 'Enchantress' was a day cruiser with accommodation on the deck (note the basket chairs and canvas deck chairs) as well as in the cabin. The 'Silver Swallow' was a two-cabin luxury cruiser whose moveable canopy gave shelter from sun or rain to the helmsman. Both boats are flying the standard of Robinsons Boatyard.

Brundall, A Backwater c1960 B497005
A backwater where several interesting craft are moored. On the left is a wartime landing craft, which has been converted into a houseboat. Next to it, the yacht has a deep hull, indicating that it is a sea-going boat not primarily intended for use on the broads. The small boats on the right are old punts, the kind used by wild fowlers.

Fleet Dyke

The Broads
Fleet Dyke c1934 T213091
The Fleet Dyke flows into the river Yare at Breydon Water just short of Great Yarmouth. A break in the storm cloud allows the evening sun to cast shadows on the rippling water, a sight not uncommon on the Broads. This photograph shows two yachts moored for the night in the somewhat bleak area of Halvergate Marshes.

The Broads
Fleet Dyke c1955
T213038
The Dyke is here almost as wide as a river, and allows a sail cruiser to tack across. Several holidaymakers on a hired motor cruiser watch the skilful sailing manoeuvre. The child sitting on the cabin roof appears to be wearing a lifejacket.

◄ **Loddon, The Basin c1965** L369014

By 1965 most of the boats on the Broads were motorised. The lifebelt on the left of the picture is a reminder that each year the Broads claim lives. Not only do currents sweep under the boats, but there is a great danger of becoming entangled with weeds below the surface. Hire boat companies now issue life jackets as a matter of course.

Loddon

Loddon lies on the south side of the river Chet. Over the road bridge, on the opposite bank, is the mainly residential village of Chedgrave.

Loddon, High Street and the Town Sign c1955
L369004
Except for the proliferation of telephone lines and TV aerials, this view up the main street of Loddon might have been photographed today. The petrol station, with pumps delivering fuel from different suppliers, has been replaced by houses, but the Pedlar still surveys the rows of Georgian houses and shops from the town sign.

Loddon The Riverside c1965
L369020
Here we see a busy scene, with many hire boats waiting to be refuelled at the pump and taken out into the river. Aston Boats' Nissen huts have now been taken over by Princess Cruisers, and the sheds alongside the moorings have been replaced by a house.

Chedgrave
The Church c1955 C717008
Separated from Loddon by the river Chet, the village of Chedgrave has become a desirable residential area. All Saints' Church stands solidly against the east wind which blows across the marshes. A meeting room has been added on to the west end of the tiny church. The unusual square tower at the north-east corner is thatched with Norfolk reed.

The River Waveney

Traditionally marking the border between Norfolk and Suffolk, the river Waveney qualifies as part of the Norfolk Broads as it joins the Yare at Burgh Castle to flow into Breydon Water and out into the North Sea at Yarmouth.

Beccles

Beccles
The Boathouse 1894 33349
The tranquillity of reed beds and alder carr fringing a quiet backwater near Beccles is being enjoyed by the man relaxing in his wide-bottomed dinghy. Note his formal dress, with hat and waistcoat, and the padded seat for a passenger.

EAST SUFFOLK GAZETTE
WELSBACH

Beccles Market Square 1900
45096
Shopkeepers have shielded their goods from the sun's damaging rays with canvas blinds, while the donkey waits patiently. The 18th-century buildings have changed little since 1900, and the delicate wrought iron balcony can still be admired above the centre shop. Beccles Tower, adjacent to the church, was bought by the town in 1972 for one Beccles penny, but over £68,000 was needed to restore it!

◄ **Lowestoft, The Yacht Basin c1960** L105142
Yachts and motor launches idle in the Yacht Basin under the gaze of the Royal Norfolk and Suffolk Yacht Club, housed in the startling white building at the end of the harbour. There is one motor launch in the foreground and another on the right of the picture.

Lowestoft

Lowestoft, The Yacht Basin and the Harbour 1921 71699
Private yachts are moored with their dinghies alongside the basin wall. Two paddle steamers are berthed on the opposite quay, and in the centre of the picture a lady is being rowed down to the river. We can just see the swing bridge in the background. Note the unusual buoys to which some of the yachts are tied.

Lowestoft, The Pier the Miniature Railway c1955 L105076
The imposing Royal Norfolk and Suffolk Yacht Club stands sentinel at the entrance to Lowestoft pier as holidaymakers enjoy a ride in the open carriages pulled by a miniature locomotive steaming along to the end of the pier. An old man is pushed in his wheelchair, and two infants ride in an early folding perambulator.

Lowestoft
The Bridge and the Harbour c1925
L105501

It is always a sight worth watching, as the bridge swings open to allow the passage of a paddle steamer. Note the tramlines visible on the roadway of the bridge. This view of the harbour and its buildings has changed little in the last 80 years, but a new lifting bridge, with a 3-lane highway and 2 pedestrian walkways, has replaced this old swing bridge.

Great Yarmouth

Great Yarmouth is a busy seaside resort and trading port where the Bure, the Waveney and the Yare merge to flow into the North Sea. It was formerly a major fishing port, but the herring fleet has now disappeared.

Great Yarmouth, The River Yare 1887 19873
This early photograph shows wooden sailing cruisers moored alongside the jetty. The river at this point is wide and tidal. The busy industrial town can be seen on the opposite bank.

Great Yarmouth
The Town Hall 1922
72536
A solid example of Victorian civic architecture, Yarmouth Town Hall stands squarely alongside the quay. A paddle steamer, crowded with holidaymakers, awaits more passengers. It carries two lifeboats and several lifebelts.

Great Yarmouth
From Britannia Pier 1899 44495

Holiday makers in deck chairs are all fully dressed. A few children are paddling in the sea, but there no swimmers, although rows of bathing machines are set up along the shore. The wind is already whipping the half-hoisted sail of a pleasure boat as it waits for more passengers to board along the walkway.

Index

FRITH PRODUCTS & SERVICES

Francis Frith would doubtless be pleased to know that the pioneering publishing venture he started in 1860 still continues today. Over a hundred and forty years later, The Francis Frith Collection continues in the same innovative tradition and is now one of the foremost publishers of vintage photographs in the world. Some of the current activities include:

INTERIOR DECORATION

Today Frith's photographs can be seen framed and as giant wall murals in thousands of pubs, restaurants, hotels, banks, retail stores and other public buildings throughout the country. In every case they enhance the unique local atmosphere of the places they depict and provide reminders of gentler days in an increasingly busy and frenetic world.

PRODUCT PROMOTIONS

Frith products are used by many major companies to promote the sales of their own products or to reinforce their own history and heritage. Frith promotions have been used by Hovis bread, Courage beers, Scots Porage Oats, Colman's mustard, Cadbury's foods, Mellow Birds coffee, Dunhill pipe tobacco, Guinness, and Bulmer's Cider.

GENEALOGY AND FAMILY HISTORY

As the interest in family history and roots grows world-wide, more and more people are turning to Frith's photographs of Great Britain for images of the towns, villages and streets where their ancestors lived; and, of course, photographs of the churches and chapels where their ancestors were christened, married and buried are an essential part of every genealogy tree and family album.

FRITH PRODUCTS

All Frith photographs are available Framed or just as Mounted Prints and Posters (size 23 x 16 inches). These may be ordered from the address below. Other products available are - Address Books, Calendars, Jigsaws, Canvas Prints, Postcards and local and prestige books.

THE INTERNET

Already ninety thousand Frith photographs can be viewed and purchased on the internet through the Frith websites and a myriad of partner sites.

For more detailed information on Frith products, look at this site:
www.francisfrith.com

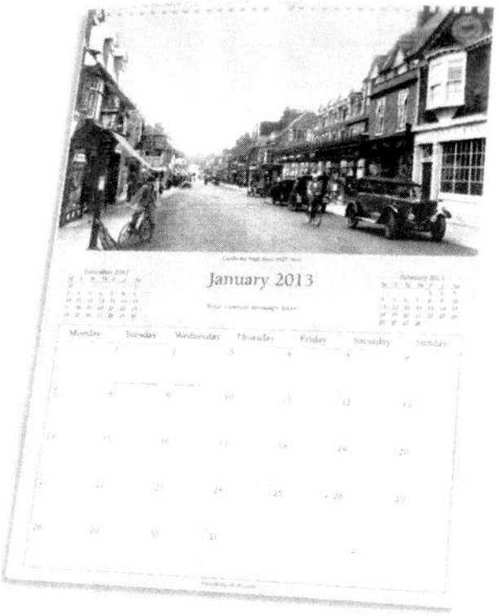

See the complete list of Frith Books at: www.francisfrith.com
This web site is regularly updated with the latest list of publications from The Francis Frith Collection. If you wish to buy books relating to another part of the country that your local bookshop does not stock, you may purchase on-line.

For further information, trade, or author enquiries please contact us at the address below:
The Francis Frith Collection, Unit 6, Oakley Business Park, Wylye Road, Dinton, Wiltshire SP3 5EU.
Tel: +44 (0)1722 716 376 Fax: +44 (0)1722 716 881 Email: sales@francisfrith.co.uk

See Frith products on the internet at www.francisfrith.com

FREE PRINT OF YOUR CHOICE
CHOOSE A PHOTOGRAPH FROM THIS BOOK

+ £3.80 POSTAGE

Mounted Print
Overall size 14 x 11 inches (355 x 280mm)

TO RECEIVE YOUR FREE PRINT

Choose any Frith photograph in this book

Simply complete the Voucher opposite and return it with your remittance for £3.50 (to cover postage and handling) and we will print the photograph of your choice in SEPIA (size 11 x 8 inches) and supply it in a cream mount ready to frame (overall size 14 x 11 inches).

Order additional Mounted Prints at HALF PRICE - £12.00 each (normally £24.00)

If you would like to order more Frith prints from this book, possibly as gifts for friends and family, you can buy them at half price (with no additional postage costs).

Have your Mounted Prints framed

For an extra £20.00 per print you can have your mounted print(s) framed in an elegant polished wood and gilt moulding, overall size 16 x 13 inches (no additional postage required).

IMPORTANT!

1. Please note: aerial photographs and photographs with a reference number starting with a "Z" are not Frith photographs and cannot be supplied under this offer.
2. Offer valid for delivery to one UK address only.
3. These special prices are only available if you use this form to order. You must use the ORIGINAL VOUCHER on this page (no copies permitted). We can only despatch to one UK address.
4. This offer cannot be combined with any other offer.

As a customer your name & address will be stored by Frith but not sold or rented to third parties. Your data will be used for the purpose of this promotion only.

Send completed Voucher form to:

The Francis Frith Collection,
19 Kingsmead Business Park, Gillingham,
Dorset SP8 5FB

Voucher *for* ***FREE*** *and Reduced Price Frith Prints*

Please do not photocopy this voucher. Only the original is valid, so please fill it in, cut it out and return it to us with your order.

Picture ref no	Page no	Qty	Mounted @ £12.00	Framed + £20.00	Total Cost £
		1	Free of charge*	£	£
			£12.00	£	£
			£12.00	£	£
			£12.00	£	£
			£12.00	£	£
			£12.00	£	£
			* Post & handling		£3.80
			Total Order Cost		£

Please allow 28 days for delivery.
Offer available to one UK address only

Title of this book . . . .

I enclose a cheque/postal order for £ . . . .
made payable to 'The Francis Frith Collection'

OR please debit my Mastercard / Visa / Maestro card, details below

Card Number:

Issue No (Maestro only): Valid from (Maestro):

Card Security Number: Expires:

Signature:

Name Mr/Mrs/Ms ....

Address ....

....

....

.... Postcode ....

Daytime Tel No ....

Email ....

Valid to 31/12/18

Free Print - see overleaf

Can you help us with information about any of the Frith photographs in this book?

We are gradually compiling an historical record for each of the photographs in the Frith archive. It is always fascinating to find out the names of the people shown in the pictures, as well as insights into the shops, buildings and other features depicted.

If you recognize anyone in the photographs in this book, or if you have information not already included in the author's caption, do let us know. We would love to hear from you, and will try to publish it in future books or articles.

An Invitation from The Francis Frith Collection to Share Your Memories

The 'Share Your Memories' feature of our website allows members of the public to add personal memories relating to the places featured in our photographs, or comment on others already added. Seeing a place from your past can rekindle forgotten or long held memories. Why not visit the website, find photographs of places you know well and add YOUR story for others to read and enjoy? We would love to hear from you!

www.francisfrith.com/memories

Our production team

Frith books are produced by a small dedicated team at offices near Salisbury. Most have worked with the Frith Collection for many years. All have in common one quality: they have a passion for the Frith Collection.

Frith Books and Gifts

We have a wide range of books and gifts available on our website utilising our photographic archive, many of which can be individually personalised.

www.francisfrith.com

FF017914